KINDNESS

How Can We Make This World A Better Place?

LAURA PRESTON-JACKSON

To order additional copies of this book, contact:
Xlibris
844-714-8691
www.Xlibris.com
Orders@Xlibris.com

ISBN: 978-1-6698-6284-0 (sc)
ISBN: 978-1-6698-6618-3 (e)

Print information available on the last page

Rev. date: 08/29/2023

Hugs and kisses to my amazing village.

I am grateful to my parents Steve and Elizabeth Preston; my wonderful children AJ and Lauren; and my beautiful sisters Lisa (my twin) and Lynn.

"Kindness is a gift everyone can afford to give."

-Unknown

KINDNESS

How can we make this world a better place?

Kindness is selfless, compassionate and merciful.

Kindness is **love**.

The Cambridge Dictionary defines kindness as the quality of being generous, helpful and caring about other people or an act showing it.

"Kindness is the language that the deaf can hear and the blind can see. It can transverse boundaries, race, and even disabilities."

Mark Twain

Here is how we can make this
world a better place . . .

by showing kindness.

Kindness is free!

Kindness is caring

. . . Are you alright?

. . . Do you need some help?

Kindness lends a helping hand

. . . I'll help you!

. . . Do you need a hand with that?

. . . Plays fairly.

When you're kind to others, you can
get along and play together.

When you are kind to others, speak kind words.

Hi, how are you today?

I like your watch!

Your hair is so pretty!

Kindness lights up a room
with your presence.

Kindness is letting someone
go ahead of you in line.

It says *"Please"* and *"Thank you!"*

Kindness invites the odd one out, *in.*

Kindness is . . .

helping a friend when others are being mean.

Kindness is saying kind words when someone is feeling sad.

Kindness speaks good words about you.

That's pretty!

Glad to see you today.

Kindness does and says things on purpose.

A kind person will find something *good* to say
even if you have to look very hard.

Kindness apologizes no matter what.

I'm sorry!

Please forgive me.

Kindness speaks in everything you do and in every language.

Your kindness will cheer up someone
who is sad or having a rough day.

Kindness is being concerned about the feelings of others.

Kindness is being nice even when others are not.

. . . Would you like to play with us?

. . . Sit with us at lunch!

Kindness is a verb.

Verbs are words that show action.

Action is doing!

Kindness is a movement.

Has someone ever done something kind to you and all you wanted to do after was pay it forward? That's because kindness is a chain reaction. It's a wave that keeps rolling, and all it needs is one person to start it. One small act of kindness can cause a ripple effect that impacts an entire community. If we are all focused on being kind, we are creating a movement of change.

You know the famous quote is "be the change you wish to see in the world!" That quote isn't just about change, and it isn't only about one person being able to change their world. It's bigger; it's about a movement that can be started from one person acting with intention.

You can show kindness each day with a simple **"hello."**

Speaking to someone lets them know that you see them.

Kindness is caring enough to share.

Kindness is helping someone by volunteering to take over a push.

Kindness are deeds shown to let someone know _you care_, _love_, and _respect_ them.

Kindness comes in all colors and languages.

Kindness wears a smile

. . . Watching you smile makes me smile.

We can show kindness everywhere we go by . . .

Giving a hug to a friend

Opening the door for someone

Giving a compliment

Helping someone carry things
when they need help

Doing your chore when asked

Taking food to someone who is sick.

Kindness says "I'm sorry!"

Kindness brings an extra treat to a friend.

Kindness makes a card and sends it to soldiers or someone helping our country.

Kindness donates toys to other kids in need.

If you want to make this world a better place,

...tell someone how much you appreciate them.

...write a note of thanks.

...write a letter to your parents thanking them for all they do.

...tell a family member or a friend "I love you."

...help your neighbor with their yard work.

...tell the truth.

Kindness is grace.

Merriam-Webster defines it as a person having grace, to be one with a controlled, polite, and pleasant way of behaving.

When you think of Kindness think of.....

A is for affection

B is for behavior

C is for considerate

D is for dignity

E is for effort

F is for friendly

G is for giving

H is for heart-warming

I is for intergrity

J is for joy

K is for kindhearted

L is for loving

M is for merciful

N is for nice

O is for openness

P is for patience

Q is for quaint

R is for real

S is for smile

T is for thoughtfulness

U is for understanding

V is for vulnerable

W is for willingness

X is for eXcited

Y is for yielding

Z is for Zeal

K is for kindhearted.

I is for integrity.

N is for just be *nice!*

D is for dignity.

Kindness will always win.

Printed in the United States
by Baker & Taylor Publisher Services